Camille Saint-Saëns

Introduction et Rondo capriccioso
for Violin and Orchestra / für Violine und Orchester
Op. 28

Havanaise
for Violin and Orchestra / für Violine und Orchester
Op. 83

Edited by / Herausgegeben von
Wolfgang Birtel

T0081235

Eulenburg

EAS 191
ISBN 978-3-7957-6591-0
ISMN 979-0-2002-2622-5
© 2014 Ernst Eulenburg & Co GmbH, Mainz
for Europe excluding the British Isles
Ernst Eulenburg Ltd, London
for all other countries
CD ℗ 1994 & 2003 NAXOS Rights US, Inc.
CD © 2014 Ernst Eulenburg Ltd, London

Ernst Eulenburg Ltd
48 Great Marlborough Street
London W1F 7BB

Contents / Inhalt

Andante (malinconico)

Allegro ma non troppo

Allegretto lusinghiero

Preface

Introduction et Rondo capriccioso
Composed: 1863
First performance: 1867, Théâtre des Champs-Élysées;
soloist: Pablo de Sarasate
Original publisher: Durand & Fils, Paris
Instrumentation: 2 Flutes, 2 Oboes, 2 Clarinets, 2 Bassoons – 2 Horns,
2 Trumpets – Timpani – Strings
Duration: ca. 9 minutes

Havanaise
Composed: 1887
First performance: 1888 (?), Musik-Institut Koblenz;
soloist: Rafael Diaz Albertini
Original publisher: Durand & Fils, Paris
Instrumentation: 2 Flutes, 2 Oboes, 2 Clarinets, 2 Bassoons – 2 Horns,
2 Trumpets – Timpani – Strings
Duration: ca. 10 minutes

'Oddly enough, you can talk with musicians for hours about the music of France, yet it would never occur to anyone to mention the name Saint-Saëns.'[1] Thus the French writer and music critic Romain Rolland expressed his bewilderment at Saint-Saëns' neglect in turn-of-the-century France, a sentiment that reflects the country's general ambivalence towards her most Romantic composer. During his lifetime, Saint-Saëns initially enjoyed great popularity but was later despised, opposed and finally ignored by his countrymen; this was due not least to the fact that he was never part of a particular movement or school but remained true to his own aesthetic ideals and compositional style. As a result, works that had once seemed new and even revolutionary were decades later decried as reactionary. Outside France, however, Saint-Saëns was able to establish a reputation for himself, his music increasingly appreciated, except for those two periods when wartime tensions caused his music to fall from favour, in 1870–71 and again from 1914 to 1918.

---

[1] Quoted by Michael Stegemann, *Camille Saint-Saëns und das französische Solokonzert von 1850 bis 1920* (Mainz, 1984), 10; trans. Ann C. Sherwin as *Camille Saint-Saëns and the French Solo Concerto from 1850 to 1920* (Portland, Oregon, 1991), 18. Stegemann's study continues to offer the best overview of the composer's concertante output.

Writing in the *Revue blanche* on 15 November 1901, Claude Debussy noted that his fellow composer 'knows the musical universe better than anyone else'.[2] Few other composers, it may be added, have left such an extensive and comprehensive corpus of works. Not only did Saint-Saëns write symphonic and dramatic music, vocal and chamber works, piano music, military band music and ballet music, but also the first original soundtrack for a film, *L'Assassinat du Duc de Guise* (1908). He wrote concertos and solo pieces throughout his long life, from the Violin Concerto in C major Op.58 (1858), later officially designated his Second Violin Concerto, to his Second Cello Concerto in D minor Op.119 of 1902. The concerto genre as a whole owed a great deal to Saint-Saëns, for it had lost much of its prestige in 19th-century France and become the poor cousin of serious music, having sunk to the level of a purely virtuosic display vehicle with the orchestra merely providing backing for the soloist's brilliant pyrotechnics. Everything that departed from the three-movement norm and from the orchestra's subordinate function, anything that distracted the audience from the soloist's performance was found to be puzzling and even disturbing by audiences and critics alike. Saint-Saëns' concertos were therefore bound to encounter resistance, for not only did they flout all formal expectations but they created a new and more balanced relationship between the solo instrument and the orchestra, thereby challenging the soloist's previous predominance. And yet so egregious did their perceived shortcomings appear that performances of these concertos were greeted by vociferous protests and derided by many of the critics of the time. Critical reactions to the larger concerto form were reflected – though perhaps not so dramatically – in attitudes towards smaller works, salon music and bravura pieces, too.

Saint-Saëns favoured the violin repertoire in particular with two sonatas, three concertos and a series of smaller works with piano or orchestral accompaniment. Some of the inspiration for these doubtless came from his friendship with the Spanish violinist Pablo de Sarasate, who delighted audiences with his circus tricks and his sweetly languishing tone on the violin. Sarasate gave Saint-Saëns many tips as to what was technically possible on the violin – and the composer dedicated his first and third violin concertos and the *Introduction et Rondo capriccioso* to him. 'With his magical bow Pablo de Sarasate took my compositions all over the world and thereby did me the greatest service possible', wrote Saint-Saëns on 15 October 1908 in an article for the *Revue Musicale* (*Revue d'Histoire et de critique musicale*).[3] It is doubtless also from his acquaintance with Sarasate that the composer acquired a fondness for Spanish tone colour and folk tunes, most clearly felt in the *Introduction et Rondo capriccioso* Op.28, in the *Havanaise* Op.83 and in the *Caprice andalou* Op.122.

Saint-Saëns had a visit from the 15-year-old Sarasate in 1859: 'Some time ago now', the composer later recalled, 'the already famous Pablo de Sarasate came to see me one day. He was young and fresh as Spring. [...] Very sweetly, as though it were the simplest thing in the world, he asked me to write a concerto for him. I was deeply flattered and so captivated by him that I gave him my promise – and I kept my word with the Violin Concerto in A major.

---

[2] Claude Debussy, *Monsieur Croche et autres écrits*, ed. François Lesure (Paris, 1987), 57; trans. Richard Langham Smith as *Debussy on Music: The Critical Writings of the Great French Composer* (Ithaca, New York, 1977), 54

[3] Quoted from: Charles-Camille Saint-Saëns, *Musikalische Reminiszenzen*, ed. Reiner Zimmermann (Leipzig, 1978), 130

[...] I also wrote the *Rondo capriccioso* in Spanish style for him, and later the Concerto in B minor'.[4] *Introduction et Rondo capriccioso* was written in 1863. At the time Saint-Saëns was earning his living as organist at the *Église de la Madeleine* in Paris and teaching piano, while also active as a pianist and composer. His creative efforts had yet to meet with critical approval: 'Monsieur Saint-Saëns imagines that it will suffice to mislead connoisseurs if he just cobbles together some scheme or other for hammering out harsh chords on the piano. So far, he has not managed to convince us that God intended him to compose music', wrote a critic in the *Revue des Deux Mondes* on 15 June 1862.[5]

*

Introduction et Rondo capriccioso was then and remains today a highlight of the Romantic violin repertoire. Saint-Saëns described the piece as 'composed in the Spanish style': such exotic touches were very popular with audiences at that time and the composer was happy to oblige with a number of pieces including a *Caprice arabe*, *Suite algérienne*, *Jota aragonese*, a piano fantasia *Africa* and other works besides. The first performance of the *Rondo* and the first Violin Concerto on 4 April 1867 at the *Théâtre des Champs-Élysées* played by Pablo de Sarasate and conducted by Saint-Saëns finally brought him some recognition as a composer. The *Revue et Gazette musicale* praised his writing for the violin and commented that 'Monsieur Saint-Saëns knows the violin's whole range of effects as well as any violinist and furthermore has the ability to show off its capabilities with an accompaniment that remains interesting throughout. The main feature of the concert, however, was a new Violin Concerto in A, masterfully performed by Monsieur Sarasate.'[6] Originally conceived as a final movement for the Violin Concerto No.1 in A major Op.20, the Finale proved so popular that the composer decided to publish it separately. *Introduction et Rondo capriccioso* was published in 1870, scored for piano and violin – the piano part in fact arranged by Georges Bizet; orchestral parts and a full score followed in 1875 and 1879. An introductory recitative alternates between lyrical and playful passages which lead into the Rondo, where the composer gives the violin an opportunity for a furious technical firework display: this is an effective bravura piece to show off the abilities of any virtuoso violinist.

*

At the beginning of the 1880s Saint-Saëns' popularity abroad spilled over to the French capital: his election to the *Académie des Beaux-Arts* of the *Institut de France* (1881) and nomination for the award of *Officier de la Légion d'honneur* (1884) were outward signs of this success. Triumphs followed on the operatic stage, too, where previously success had eluded him. In the autumn of 1885 the composer set off on a concert tour travelling through northern France with the Cuban violinist Diaz Albertini, who had trained at the Paris Conservatoire. On a cold wet evening, the crackling of a fire in the hearth of a desolate hotel in Brest is said

---

4 ibid.
5 Quoted from: Michael Stegemann, *Saint-Saëns* (Reinbek, near Hamburg, 1988), 27
6 Quoted from: Stegemann, *Solokonzert*, 18

to have inspired him to write a melody that he incorporated in his *Havanaise* two years later.[7] Indeed, he dedicated this work to Albertini, his companion on the tour, who had also contributed a musical suggestion of his own. It was published in 1888 in a version for violin and piano; the composer orchestrated the original piano accompaniment soon afterwards at the request of the publisher, as Sarasate wanted to perform the work in London. His preferred ensemble was '*un petit orchestre à l'eau de rose*' ('a little palm court orchestra') without trombones, for the sake of the violinists, '*qui auraient moins de son que de talent*' ('who might not be as loud as they are talented'), as he wrote to his publisher from Algiers on 21 February 1888.[8] There is no record of the work actually having been first performed by Sarasate; in fact it was probably first played by the dedicatee Diaz Albertini at a concert on 26 October 1888, the first in a series of subscription concerts at the Music Institute in Koblenz under the direction of the Polish conductor Rafał Maszkowski.[9] In this *Habanera*, a Spanish dance of Cuban origin, the composer lets the violin wallow in captivating melodies, while faster passages in this delightful gem also provide ample opportunity for displaying virtuoso technique.

Wolfgang Birtel
Translation: Julia Rushworth

---

[7] A detailed account of its genesis appears in: Camille Saint-Saëns, *Havanaise pour violon avec accompagnement de piano op. 83*, ed. Christine Baur (Kassel, Basel etc., 2012), IIIf.

[8] Sabina Teller Ratner: *Camille Saint-Saëns 1835–1921. A Thematic Catalogue of his Complete Works, Vol. I: The Instrumental Works*, Oxford 2002, 389

[9] S. Baur, IV. The author here revises information given in the index of works, which details a first performance in Paris on 7 January 1894 in the concert series *Concerts Colonne* at the *Théâtre du Châtelet* with soloist Martin-Pierre Marsick, conductor Édouard Colonne and his orchestra.

Vorwort

Introduction et Rondo capriccioso
komponiert: 1863
Uraufführung: 1867 im Théâtre des Champs-Élysées;
Solist: Pablo de Sarasate
Originalverlag: Durand & Fils, Paris
Orchesterbesetzung: 2 Flöten, 2 Oboen, 2 Klarinetten, 2 Fagotte –
2 Hörner, 2 Trompeten – Pauken – Streicher
Spieldauer: etwa 9 Minuten

Havanaise
komponiert: 1887
Uraufführung: 1888 (?), Musik-Institut Koblenz;
Solist: Rafael Diaz Albertini
Originalverlag: Durand & Fils, Paris
Orchesterbesetzung: 2 Flöten, 2 Oboen, 2 Klarinetten, 2 Fagotte –
2 Hörner, 2 Trompeten – Pauken – Streicher
Spieldauer: etwa 10 Minuten

„Es ist sonderbar: Man kann stundenlang mit Musikern über die Musik Frankreichs sprechen, doch nie fiele es einem ein, den Namen Saint-Saëns zu erwähnen", wunderte sich der französische Schriftsteller und Musikkritiker Romain Rolland einmal[1] – seine Verwunderung spiegelt die ambivalente Haltung Frankreichs ihrem romantischen Komponisten gegenüber deutlich wider: Zu Lebzeiten erfreute er sich zunächst großer Beliebtheit, wurde dann aber verachtet, bekämpft, totgeschwiegen; auch, weil er sich keiner Strömung oder Schule anschloss, seinen ästhetischen Ansichten und seinem Kompositionsstil treu blieb. Und so kam es, dass seine Werke zunächst neu, ja revolutionär wirkten, Jahrzehnte später aber als reaktionär verschrien waren. Im Ausland konnte sich Camille Saint-Saëns dagegen etablieren, gewann der Musiker zusehends an Anerkennung – sieht man einmal von den deutsch-französischen „Verstimmungen" während der Kriegsjahre 1870/71 sowie 1914–18 ab.

„Saint-Saëns ist [...] ein Mann, der die Musik in- und auswendig kennt wie kein anderer", lobte Claude Debussy in der *Revue blanche* vom 15. November 1901 seinen Komponisten-

---

[1] Zit. nach Michael Stegemann: *Camille Saint-Saëns und das französische Solokonzert von 1850 bis 1920*, Mainz 1984, S. 10. Es bietet im Übrigen den besten Einblick in das konzertante Œuvre des Komponisten.

kollegen,[2] und nur wenige, darf man hinzufügen, haben ein derartig umfangreiches und alle Gattungen abdeckendes Gesamtwerk hinterlassen wie er: Symphonische und dramatische Musik, Vokal- und Kammermusik, Klavier-, Militär- und Ballettmusik hat Camille Saint-Saëns komponiert, aber auch mit *L'Assassinat du Duc de Guise* 1908 die erste originale Filmmusik geliefert. Der Komposition von Solokonzerten und Solo-„Piècen" widmete er sich zeit seines Lebens: vom Violinkonzert in C-Dur opus 58 (1858), das später die offizielle Nummer 2 erhielt, bis zu seinem zweiten Violoncellokonzert in d-Moll opus 119 (1902). Saint-Saëns verdankt die Gattung des Konzertes wesentliche Impulse, hatte sie doch im 19. Jahrhundert in Frankreich erheblich an Ansehen verloren, war zum Stiefkind kompositorischer Beschäftigung geworden: Solokonzerte waren zum reinen Virtuosenstück herabgesunken, ihr kompositorisches Ziel war es in erster Linie, dem brillierenden Solisten eine Orchester-Klangfolie zu bieten. Alles, was von der dreisätzigen Normalform und der untergeordneten Orchesterfunktion abwich, was die Aufmerksamkeit vom Solisten ablenkte, irritierte das Publikum (und die Musikkritik) oder störte gar. Da mussten die Solokonzerte von Saint-Saëns Anstoß erregen, denn einerseits durchbrachen sie den formalen Schematismus, andererseits brachten sie die absolute Vorherrschaft des Soloinstruments über den Orchesterpart in ein neues, nun ausgewogeneres Verhältnis – so sehr, dass es nicht nur zu Kritikerverrissen, sondern auch zu lautstarken Skandalaufführungen kommen sollte. Und was für die Großform des Konzertes galt, war sicher – wenn auch nicht so gravierend – für die kleineren Werke, die Salon- und Bravourstücke, von Bedeutung.

Das Geigenrepertoire hat der französische Musiker besonders bedacht: mit zwei Sonaten, drei Konzerten und einer Reihe kleinerer Werke mit Klavier- oder Orchesterbegleitung. Dazu trug sicher auch die Freundschaft mit dem spanischen Geiger Pablo de Sarasate bei, der das Publikum mit seinen zirzensischen Kunststücken und seinem süß-schmachtenden Ton auf der Violine verzückte. Er gab Saint-Saëns so manchen Tipp, was auf der Geige technisch möglich ist – ihm widmete er auch sein erstes und drittes Violinkonzert sowie *Introduction et Rondo capriccioso.* „Mit seinem Zauberbogen brachte Pablo de Sarasate meine Kompositionen durch alle Länder, und dies war von allen Diensten der ausgezeichnetste, den er mir hatte erweisen können", schrieb Camille Saint-Saëns in einem Artikel vom 15. Oktober 1908 für die *Revue Musicale* (*Revue d'Histoire et de critique musicale*).[3] Sicherlich rührt von der Bekanntschaft mit dem Geiger auch des Komponisten Faible für spanisches Kolorit, für die Folklore des Nachbarlandes her, das am deutlichsten in *Introduction et Rondo capriccioso,* opus 28, in der *Havanaise,* opus 83, und in der *Caprice andalou,* opus 122, zu spüren ist.

Der erst fünfzehnjährige Sarasate hatte 1859 Saint-Saëns aufgesucht: „Es ist ziemlich lange her", berichtete der Komponist später, „daß der schon berühmte Pablo de Sarasate eines Tages bei mir erschien. Jung und frisch wie der Frühling war er. [...] Er bat mich höchst liebenswürdig und so, als sei es die einfachste Sache von der Welt, für ihn ein Konzert zu schreiben. Ich war sehr geschmeichelt und dazu von ihm äußerst bezaubert, also gab ich ihm

---

[2] Zit. nach Claude Debussy: *Monsieur Croche. Sämtliche Schriften und Interviews,* hrsg. v. François Lesure. Aus dem Französischen übertr. v. Josef Häusler, Stuttgart 1974, S. 54.

[3] Zit. nach: Charles-Camille Saint-Saëns: *Musikalische Reminiszenzen,* hrsg. v. Reiner Zimmermann, Leipzig 1978, S. 130.

mein Versprechen, und ich hielt mein Wort mit dem Violinkonzert A-Dur. [...] Ich habe danach noch das ,Rondo capriccioso' in spanischem Stil und später das Konzert h-Moll für ihn geschrieben".[4] *Introduction et Rondo capriccioso* entstand im Jahre 1863. Der Musiker verdiente sich zu dieser Zeit seinen Unterhalt als Organist an der Pariser *Église de la Madeleine* und als Klavierlehrer, war daneben aber auch als Pianist und Komponist tätig. Doch seine kreativen Bemühungen fanden noch wenig positive Resonanz: „Monsieur Saint-Saëns bildet sich ein, es würde genügen, nach irgendeinem aufgegabelten Rezept grelle Akkorde auf dem Klavier zu hämmern, um die Kenner irrezuführen. Bis jetzt ist es ihm noch nicht gelungen, uns davon zu überzeugen, daß Gott ihn dazu bestimmt hat, Musik zu komponieren", urteilte die *Revue des Deux Mondes* noch am 15. Juni 1862.[5]

*

Introduction et Rondo capriccioso ist damals wie heute ein Highlight im romantischen Violinrepertoire. Als „in spanischem Stil" komponiert bezeichnete der Komponist das Werk ausdrücklich: Solche Exotismen gefielen dem damaligen Publikum ausgesprochen gut und der Komponist „bediente" die Erwartungen mit etlichen Werken, mit einer *Caprice arabe*, einer *Suite algérienne*, einer *Jota aragonese*, einer Klavierfantasie *Africa* und anderen Opera mehr. Die Uraufführung des Rondos und des ersten Violinkonzertes am 4. April 1867 im *Théâtre des Champs-Élysées* mit Pablo de Sarasate und Saint-Saëns am Dirigentenpult brachte ihm endlich auch einmal Anerkennung als Komponist. Die *Revue et Gazette musicale* lobte die Violinkomposition und berichtete: „Monsieur Saint-Saëns kennt alle Effekte der Violine und ihren ganzen Reichtum ebenso gut wie jeder Geiger und hat obendrein auch das Können, sie durch eine stets interessante Begleitung hervorzuheben. – Der ,größte Brocken' des Konzerts aber war ein neues Violinkonzert in A, das Monsieur Sarasate meisterhaft interpretierte."[6] Ursprünglich als Schluss-Satz des Violinkonzertes Nr. 1 in A-Dur opus 20 gedacht, war das Finale derart erfolgreich, dass der Komponist beschloss, es separat zu veröffentlichen. *Introduction et Rondo capriccioso* erschien 1870 als Klavierauszug mit Violine – die Klavierstimme stammte übrigens von Georges Bizet –; Orchesterstimmen und Partitur folgten 1875 und 1879. Eine rezitativische Introduktion, die zwischen lyrischen und spielerischen Passagen wechselt, leitet zum Rondo über, in dem der Komponist der Violine Gelegenheit zu einem furiosen technischen Feuerwerk gibt – ein effektvolles Bravourstück, ein Paradestück für jeden Violinvirtuosen.

*

Anfang der 1880er Jahre sollte die Wertschätzung, die Camille Saint-Saëns im Ausland erfuhr, auch auf die französische Metropole überschwappen: Die Wahl in die *Académie des beaux-arts* des *Institut de France* (1881) und die Ernennung zum *Officier de la Légion d'honneur* (1884) waren hier die äußeren Zeichen. Erfolge, nun auch auf der Opernbühne, mehrten sich – Erfolge, die ihm bislang verwehrt gewesen waren. Im Herbst 1885 startete der Musiker mit dem kubanischen, am Pariser *Conservatoire* ausgebildeten Geiger Rafael Diaz Albertini

---

[4] Ebda.
[5] Zit. nach: Michael Stegemann: *Saint-Saëns*, Reinbek bei Hamburg 1988, S. 27.
[6] Zit. nach: Stegemann, *Solokonzert*, S. 18.

zu einer Konzerttournee, die ihn in den Norden Frankreichs führte. An einem nasskalten Abend soll ihn das Knistern eines Kaminfeuers in einem trostlosen Hotel in Brest zu einem melodischen Einfall inspiriert haben, den er zwei Jahre später in seine *Havanaise* einbaute.[7] Die Komposition widmete er übrigens seinem Tourgefährten Albertini, der auch einen eigenen musikalischen Gedanken beigesteuert hatte. Sie erschien – als Violin-/Klavierversion – 1888 im Druck. Den originalen Klavierpart orchestrierte der Komponist schon bald darauf auf Bitten des Verlegers, da Sarasate das Werk in London spielen wollte. Als Besetzung wählte er „un petit orchestre à l'eau de rose" („ein kleines Kitschorchester"), ohne Posaunen, mit Rücksicht auf die Violinisten, „qui auraient moins de son que de talent" („vielleicht weniger Klang als Begabung") hätten, wie er seinem Verleger am 21. Februar 1888 in einem Brief aus Algiers mitteilte.[8] Ob Sarasate dann das Werk tatsächlich erstmals spielte, ist nicht belegt. Vermutlich war es der Widmungsträger Diaz Albertini in einem Konzert am 26. Oktober 1888 im Rahmen des ersten Abonnementskonzertes des Koblenzer Musik-Instituts unter der Leitung des polnischen Musikdirektors Rafał Maszkowski.[9] In dieser Habanera, einem spanischen Tanz kubanischer Herkunft, lässt der Komponist die Violine mit einschmeichelnden Melodien schwelgen; aber auch diesem bezaubernden Kleinod fehlt es in den schnellen Passagen nicht an virtuosem Glanz.

Wolfgang Birtel

---

[7] Eine detaillierte Entstehungsgeschichte in: Camille Saint-Saëns, *Havanaise pour violon avec accompagnement de piano op. 83*, hrsg. v. Christine Baur, Kassel, Basel usw. 2012, S. IIIf.

[8] Sabina Teller Ratner: *Camille Saint-Saëns 1835–1921. A Thematic Catalogue of his Complete Works, Vol. I: The Instrumental Works*, Oxford 2002, S. 389.

[9] S. Baur, S. IV. Die Autorin revidiert damit die Angabe des Werkverzeichnisses, das noch von einer Uraufführung in Paris am 7. Januar 1894 im Rahmen der *Concerts Colonne* im *Théâtre du Châtelet* mit dem Solisten Martin-Pierre Marsick ausging, mit Édouard Colonne am Pult seines Orchesters.

Introduction et Rondo capriccioso

Camille Saint-Saëns
(1835–1921)
Op. 28

EAS 191

Edited by Wolfgang Birtel
© 2014 Ernst Eulenburg Ltd, London
and Ernst Eulenburg & Co GmbH, Mainz

4

6

10

14

16

28

Havanaise

A Monsieur Diaz Albertini

Camille Saint-Saëns
(1835–1921)
Op. 83

EAS 191

Edited by Wolfgang Birtel
© 2014 Ernst Eulenburg Ltd, London
and Ernst Eulenburg & Co GmbH, Mainz

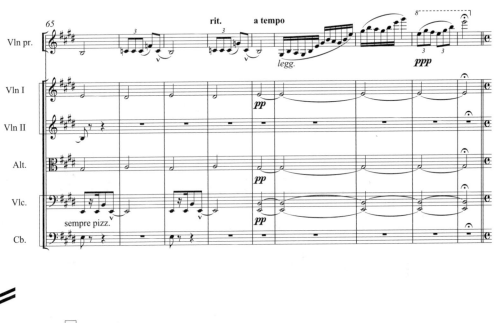

44

EAS 191

54

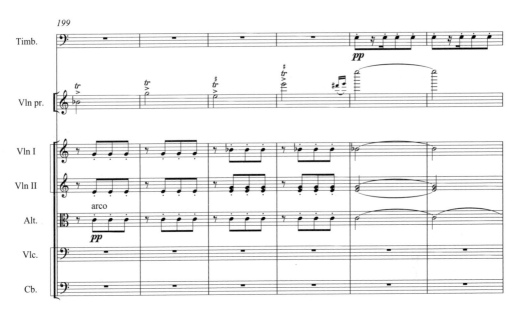

58

60

64